Eleanor Roosevelt

YEARLING BOOKS are designed especially to entertain and enlighten young people. The finest available books for children have been selected under the direction of Charles F. Reasoner, Professor of Elementary Education, New York University.

For a complete listing of all Yearling titles,
write to Education Sales Department, Dell Publishing Co., Inc.
1 Dag Hammarskjold Plaza, New York, New York 10017.

Eleanor Roosevelt
First Lady of the World

by Charles P. Graves

illustrated by Polly Bolian

A Yearling Book

For my mother-in-law,

Marian Weld Minot

Published by
DELL PUBLISHING CO., INC.
1 Dag Hammarskjold Plaza
New York, N.Y. 10017

Copyright © 1966 by Charles P. Graves

ISBN: 0-440-42238-8
Reprinted by arrangement with Garrard Publishing Co.
Printed in U.S.A.
Fifth Dell Printing—May 1977

ELEANOR ROOSEVELT is one of the *Discovery* biographies
published by Garrard Publishing Co., Champaign, Illinois.
Discovery books are published by Garrard in library bindings.

This book is one of a series of educational, informative
biographies, presented in a lively, colorful and interesting
manner. They are designed and edited so that they can be
read and enjoyed by young readers through the elementary
grades. All facts are authentic for they have been carefully
checked with leading sources for historical accuracy.

Contents

Chapter 1

Two Voyages

"Look, Eleanor." Mr. Roosevelt lifted his little girl above the ship's rail. "There's the Statue of Liberty. It was just put up last year."

Eleanor gazed at the giant statue of "Miss Liberty" holding a torch. "What a big lady!" she cried.

The year was 1887. Anna Eleanor Roosevelt was two and a half years old. She and her mother and father were on the *Britannic,* a ship that was leaving New York City for Europe.

The next day the ship ran into some heavy fog. The fog whistle blew every few seconds to warn other ships nearby.

Mr. and Mrs. Roosevelt had tea with some friends that afternoon. Eleanor passed the cake.

Mrs. Roosevelt was a very lovely woman. She thought Eleanor was an ugly duckling. "She is such a funny child," Eleanor's mother said to one of her friends. "She's so shy and so old-fashioned. We call her 'Granny.'"

Eleanor hung her head in shame. She was glad when her parents took her for a walk on deck.

The fog was so thick that Eleanor could hardly see the water. Suddenly, the fog lifted. Another ship was headed straight toward them!

With a loud noise the ship plowed into the *Britannic*. It ripped a big hole in her side.

"Stay here," Mr. Roosevelt told his family. "I'll get our life preservers."

When he returned the deck was crowded with passengers. A sailor ran up. "Lower the lifeboats!" he shouted. "The ship is sinking!"

Mr. Roosevelt was afraid to climb into a lifeboat holding Eleanor. He might drop her.

"Hold my little girl," he told one of the sailors. "Then hand her to me."

When he was in the lifeboat he held out his arms. The sailor tossed Eleanor through the air and her father caught her. Eleanor started to cry.

The ship that hit the *Britannic* was

the *Celtic*. It didn't seem to be sinking, so the men in the lifeboat rowed toward it. Sailors on the *Celtic* lifted the Roosevelts aboard.

A short time later a message came from the *Britannic*. The captain said the ship would not sink after all. But it must return to New York for repairs.

The *Celtic* was going to New York too, so the Roosevelts stayed on board.

When Eleanor was five her mother and father took her on another voyage. Her new baby brother, Elliot Roosevelt, Jr., was along too. This time the ship reached Europe safely.

The Roosevelts went to Italy, where Eleanor's father gave her a donkey. He hired a boy to lead the donkey while Eleanor rode on its back.

The boy led the donkey up a steep, rocky trail. They were gone a long time. When they returned the boy was riding on the donkey and Eleanor was leading it.

"Why aren't you riding the donkey?" Eleanor's father asked.

"Because the boy doesn't have any shoes," Eleanor said. "The rocks cut his feet and they're bleeding. I've got shoes on and I don't mind walking."

Mr. Roosevelt picked Eleanor up and hugged her. "I'm glad you're so kind and generous," he said.

Eleanor smiled. Her father always made her feel important and happy. Eleanor was never shy around him. She loved her father more than anyone else.

Chapter *2*

Orphans

While the Roosevelts were in Europe another baby was born. They named him Hall.

When they returned to New York Mr. and Mrs. Roosevelt went to many parties. One day when Eleanor was six her father asked her to go to a party. It was a Thanksgiving dinner for poor newsboys. Mr. Roosevelt wanted Eleanor to help serve the dinner at the newsboys' clubhouse.

As they rode there in a carriage, Mr. Roosevelt said, "There are many poor people in the world. It is our duty to help them." He told Eleanor that many of the newsboys were orphans and had no homes.

"Where do they sleep?" Eleanor asked.

"Sometimes in wooden boxes," Mr. Roosevelt said. "Sometimes in the door-ways of buildings."

When they reached the clubhouse it was crowded with newsboys. Eleanor saw that many of them wore rags.

She was pleased to help serve the dinner. The boys had all the turkey they could eat.

When the dinner was finished the boys put on a show. One boy stood up and told a joke. "There are two good reasons why people don't mind their own business," he began. "One is that they have no business. The other is that they have no minds."

"Ha, ha!" Eleanor giggled loudly. All the newsboys looked at her. Eleanor blushed so red that her face looked like a ripe tomato.

The newsboys sang "Yankee Doodle," and Eleanor tried to sing with them. Then she fell sound asleep and her father put her in the carriage.

The next morning Eleanor overslept and was late to school. This was unusual for her school was on the top floor of her house. Her mother and some of her friends ran the school for their children.

Sometimes when school was through

Eleanor's mother read to her. One day she was too sick to read. Doctors and nurses came to the house. The children had to be quiet all day.

Mrs. Roosevelt got worse. In a few days she died.

Eleanor's father was overcome with sorrow. He could not take care of the children. Eleanor and her two brothers went to live with their grandmother.

The next spring there was more sorrow in the family. Elliot, Jr., became ill and died.

Mr. Roosevelt came to see Eleanor and Hall whenever he could. Sometimes he took her for a ride in the park. But he was not well. Before Eleanor was 10, her father died, too.

Now Eleanor was an orphan.

Chapter **3**

Uncle Ted

Eleanor lived with her Grandmother Hall, who had one house in New York City and another one in the country. In the summer Eleanor often went to visit her father's brother, Theodore Roosevelt. She called him Uncle Ted. He lived in Oyster Bay, New York.

Uncle Ted had a big family of his own, and many nieces and nephews. The house was always full of children. Uncle Ted liked to play with the children and teach them sports.

Once the children were swimming in Oyster Bay. Uncle Ted saw Eleanor standing on the dock.

"Can't you swim, Eleanor?" he asked.

"No," Eleanor said.

"Well, jump off the dock and try."

Eleanor was afraid. But she finally got enough courage to jump. She went under the water and came up choking. Then Uncle Ted's children ducked her. Eleanor was terrified. But she loved Oyster Bay just the same.

Uncle Ted liked to chase the children through the barn. They would hide in the hay. He took them on picnics and camping trips.

When Eleanor was fifteen the visits came to an end. Her grandmother sent her to England to school.

Eleanor had never been to a real school. She soon found that she liked it. She enjoyed being with the other girls and made many friends.

While in England, Eleanor heard some exciting news about Uncle Ted. He had been elected Vice-President of the United States. William McKinley was the new President.

The next year more news came from America. President McKinley was killed by an assassin and Uncle Ted became President.

When she was seventeen Eleanor left

school and returned to America. She was a tall, shy girl who was not at all pretty. She was not very popular at dances. But people who knew her well liked her because she was so honest and sincere.

One summer day she was riding on a train in New York State. A handsome young man came up to her. "Hello, Eleanor," he said. It was her distant cousin, Franklin D. Roosevelt. "My mother is in the next car," Franklin said. "Come say hello to her."

Franklin and his mother were going to their country home at Hyde Park.

"I remember the first time you came to Hyde Park," Franklin's mother told Eleanor. "You were just a baby and Franklin rode you piggy-back."

In the months that followed Eleanor began to see more of Franklin. They often went to parties and football games together.

Franklin was a student at Harvard. He loved outdoor sports such as tennis and sailing.

When Eleanor was nineteen Franklin asked her to marry him. "You won't even have to change your last name," Franklin said.

Eleanor said she'd be delighted to marry him. But Franklin's mother thought they were too young. She made them wait. Eleanor worked in a settlement house in New York helping the poor, while Franklin finished college.

In the fall of 1904, Mrs. Roosevelt let them announce their engagement.

Another exciting thing happened that fall. Uncle Ted was elected to serve four more years as President. Eleanor asked him to give her away at her wedding.

Uncle Ted was a busy man. "I'm going to be in New York next St. Patrick's Day," he said. "Can you be married on March 17?"

"That's perfect," Eleanor said.

Early in March Uncle Ted was sworn in as President. Eleanor and Franklin went to Washington to watch.

They had seats just behind Uncle Ted. They listened to his speech. *"We have duties to others and duties to ourselves and we can shirk neither,"* they heard him say. Afterwards they went to the White House for lunch.

Two weeks after this Eleanor and Franklin were married in the home of one of Eleanor's relatives. President Roosevelt, with Eleanor on his arm, came down the stairs.

Her wedding dress was made of white satin and lace. Her veil was decorated with orange blossoms and fastened with a diamond pin.

Franklin met her at the altar.

"Dearly beloved," the minister began. When he came to the words, *"Who giveth this woman to be married to this man?"* all the wedding guests leaned forward.

Uncle Ted was supposed to push Eleanor gently ahead and place her hand in the minister's hand. Instead he said, "I do," in a loud voice.

Finally the minister pronounced Franklin and Eleanor man and wife, and the reception began. Most of the guests paid little attention to the bride and groom. They crowded around the President.

"You'd think he was the bride," Franklin said with a grin. Eleanor didn't mind. Soon she and Franklin were crowding around Uncle Ted too.

Chapter 4

A Busy Life

Franklin's mother was a rich and strong-willed woman. She still tried to make all the decisions for Franklin and Eleanor, just as if they were children.

Both Franklin and Eleanor called her "Mama." Mama expected them to spend a great deal of time with her. She gave them a house in New York City where she also had a home. Eleanor saw her every day.

Eleanor told her that she was expecting a baby. "We'll name him James," Mama said, "after my husband."

But the baby was a girl. Eleanor named her Anna Eleanor.

The next year the Roosevelts had a son and Mama had her way. They named him James. Two years later another boy was born and named Franklin, Jr. He was a big, beautiful baby, but when he was a few months old he became sick and died. Franklin helped Eleanor get over her grief.

Franklin worked in a law office. One night he told Eleanor that he didn't like his job.

"Your Uncle Ted says that the best work a man can do is to help his fellow men. I'd like to go into politics."

"Fine," Eleanor said. "If that's what you want to do, go ahead."

Franklin ran for state senator of New York on the Democratic ticket. No one thought he had much chance to win. The voters in his district were almost all Republicans.

Eleanor couldn't help him as she had a new baby and had to stay home. The baby was a boy and was called Elliot after Eleanor's father.

Franklin worked hard to win votes. He went out and met the people in his district. They liked him. The election was close, but Franklin was the winner.

In 1912, Franklin helped Woodrow Wilson run for President of the United States. Wilson won and made Franklin the Assistant Secretary of the Navy.

This was an important job. Uncle Ted had been Assistant Secretary of the Navy before he became President.

Eleanor and Franklin moved their children to Washington. Franklin often had to go on trips to inspect navy bases and ships. Sometimes Eleanor went with him.

Once she rode on a battleship that was towing a target for other ships to shoot at. The ship rose and fell on the waves. Eleanor felt seasick. She was afraid she was going to disgrace her husband.

A naval officer came up to her and pointed to the mast. "You could see the gunfire much better up there," he said. "Wouldn't you like to climb up?"

"I couldn't feel any worse up there

than I do down here," Eleanor thought. The mast was as tall as a five story building. It took her a long time to reach the top. Once she was there her seasickness left her. She had a fine view of the target practice.

While Franklin was Secretary of the Navy the Roosevelts had two more children: Franklin D. Roosevelt, Jr., and John.

Franklin's mother had given them a summer home on Campobello Island in Canada. In 1916, Eleanor took the children there for the summer. There was a terrible polio epidemic in the United States.

Franklin had to be in Washington. He wrote that the polio epidemic was *"appalling."* He was so worried about

his children's health that he wouldn't let Eleanor bring them back until the epidemic was over.

He was also worried about the war that was going on in Europe. In 1917, America entered World War I on the side of the Allies, fighting Germany.

Eleanor did a great deal of war work. She spent two or three days a week at a Red Cross canteen near the railroad station. She would help make sandwiches and coffee to give to the soldiers who came through Washington. Afterwards she often mopped the floor of the canteen.

Many soldiers and sailors who were wounded in the war were brought to hospitals in Washington. Eleanor visited them often and brought them presents.

Later she almost turned her own home into a hospital. Her husband and all five children came down with the flu at the same time. She nursed them all. She cooked their meals, made their beds, gave them their baths and took their temperatures.

Someone asked her how she could do so much, and she said, "I learned that what one has to do can be done."

Chapter *5*

Polio and Politics

In 1920 Franklin was nominated to run for Vice-President of the United States. This meant that he was one of the most important men in America. Politicians came to see him at all hours of the day and night.

One night several famous people came to dinner. Eleanor couldn't think of anything to say. She went upstairs to put the children to bed. While hearing their prayers she burst into tears. She stayed upstairs for a long time.

Franklin came up to see what was wrong.

"I just can't stand to greet all those people," Eleanor sobbed. "I know they think I'm dull and unattractive. I just want to hide up here."

"I think you're beautiful," Franklin said. "Especially when you're wearing an evening dress. Come on back downstairs."

Eleanor went and did her best.

One man who came to the house a lot was Franklin's friend and assistant, Louis Howe. At first Eleanor didn't like Louis. He was an untidy little man who smoked all the time.

Louis worked hard on Franklin's speeches. Franklin thought he was a genius. Eleanor began to respect him.

But nothing Howe or Roosevelt did could win enough votes that year. The people liked the Republican candidate for President, Warren G. Harding. The Democrats were beaten.

Louis Howe wasn't discouraged. He passed the White House and said, "That's where Franklin is going someday."

The next summer the Roosevelts went to Campobello Island as usual. They had a sailboat named the *Vireo*.

One afternoon Franklin and the three oldest children were out in the boat. Anna was fifteen now.

As the *Vireo* skimmed through the water the Roosevelts saw a forest fire on another island. They landed and fought the fire. Then they returned to Campobello.

"Let's go for a swim," Franklin said. They took a quick dip. The water felt like ice.

When they came home Franklin had a chill. The next day he was sick. His legs became paralyzed. Eleanor was terribly worried about him, but she tried not to show it.

Several doctors came to see Franklin. They didn't know what was wrong.

There were no nurses on the island. Eleanor took care of him all day long. She slept on a couch in Franklin's room.

Another doctor came to see Franklin. He said he was sure Franklin had polio. Franklin and Eleanor were afraid the children might catch the disease. But none did.

After he got better Franklin was taken to New York. He was badly crippled. He could not move his legs.

His mother wanted him to come to Hyde Park and live there like an invalid the rest of his life. She said she would take care of him.

Now for the first time Eleanor had the courage to disagree with Franklin's mother. "He must learn to take care of himself," she said. "He can still lead a useful life."

Louis Howe agreed with Eleanor. He still thought Franklin would be President some day. But Franklin was discouraged. He had loved sports. Now he couldn't even walk.

"We must get him interested in politics again," Louis said.

"How?" Eleanor asked.

"You must go into politics," Louis said. "That will get him interested again."

Eleanor started to work in the women's division of the Democratic State Committee. She brought politicians home with her to talk to Franklin. Sometimes when he talked politics he would forget that he was crippled. And Eleanor would forget that she was shy. She was getting more and more interested in politics.

Eleanor had to make some speeches. This was very hard for her. But she made herself do it. Louis Howe helped. He listened to her practice her speeches and showed her how she could be a better speaker.

She went to the New York State Democratic Convention in 1928. The Governor of New York was Alfred E. Smith. He was going to run for President.

Smith wanted Eleanor to persuade Franklin to run for Governor of New York.

"He must make his own decisions," Eleanor said. Franklin was in Warm Springs, Georgia. Swimming in the warm water there made him feel better. He still thought he might learn to walk again if he took good care of himself. It might be hard for a Governor of New York to be a cripple.

"We've tried to call him in Georgia," Smith said. "But he won't come to the phone. Will you try?"

"I'll try," Eleanor said, "but I won't try to make him change his mind."

Eleanor finally reached Franklin. "Governor Smith wants to talk to you," she said. She handed the phone to Smith and rushed out of the room to catch a train.

The next morning she read in the papers that Franklin had agreed to run for governor. It was another close election but Franklin won. The Roosevelts moved to the big Executive Mansion in Albany.

Anna was married now and had a baby. The boys were away at school and college. But when they came to Albany on weekends they made the Executive Mansion a lively place.

Chapter *6*

The White House

While Roosevelt was Governor of New York a terrible depression hit the United States. Businesses went broke. Millions of men lost their jobs. Many people didn't have enough to eat.

Mrs. Roosevelt got many letters from poor people. One old woman wrote that she was all alone except for her little dog. Now the dog was about to be taken away from her because she was

too poor to pay the tax on it. Mrs. Roosevelt paid the tax and the old woman kept her dog.

The depression became worse and worse. Banks failed and people lost all their money. More and more workers lost their jobs.

Mrs. Roosevelt's heart went out to these people. She told beggars she met on the street that they could get free meals at her house. She found jobs for many worthy people.

Eleanor was busier than ever. She taught history and government in a girls' school in New York City.

She also helped her husband in his work as governor. She traveled about the state and visited reform schools, hospitals and prisons. Then she would tell her husband what was wrong with them. He tried to make them better places.

He also tried to end the depression in New York state. But the depression was all over the country. It could not be ended in New York unless it was ended in the other states.

Franklin began to think that if he were President he could put an end to the depression throughout the nation.

Louis Howe wanted him to run for President. So did many other leaders in the Democratic Party.

Roosevelt was nominated for President at the Democratic convention in Chicago. He and Eleanor flew to Chicago. As they entered the convention hall the delegates cheered wildly.

Franklin went all over America on a campaign train. He wanted to talk to as many people as he could. Eleanor traveled with him part of the time.

Everywhere the Roosevelts went the bands played Franklin's campaign song, "Happy Days Are Here Again." The voters believed Franklin could bring happy days back to America. They elected him by millions of votes.

As soon as Franklin was elected, a reporter asked Eleanor what she was thinking.

"I am happy for my husband," she said, "because in many ways it makes up for the blow he suffered when he was stricken with infantile paralysis. And I have confidence in his ability to help the country. . . ."

Now it was Franklin's turn to be inaugurated just as Uncle Ted had been so many years before. On Inauguration Day, Eleanor rode from the White House to the Capitol with Mrs. Hoover, the wife of the outgoing President.

Mrs. Roosevelt wore a blue dress which the newspaper reporters called "Eleanor blue." The crowds cheered and waved as she went by. Eleanor waved back at the people.

After the inauguration there was a big parade. Eleanor watched it from a reviewing stand. Thousands of soldiers, led by General Douglas MacArthur, marched by.

The Roosevelts moved into the White House. Eleanor was determined to make it as cozy and informal as possible.

She insisted on running the White House elevator herself. "That just isn't done, Mrs. Roosevelt," a servant said.

"It is now," Eleanor replied with a smile.

Sometimes Eleanor took visitors on a tour of the White House. "My feeling about the White House is that it belongs to the people," she said. "Their taxes support it . . . they should be made to feel welcome here."

Chapter 7

First Lady of America

President Roosevelt had promised the people that he would try to end the depression. He got Congress to pass laws that helped banks, businesses, farmers and workers. The government hired people without jobs. These people built roads, dams, parks and public buildings.

Because the President was crippled it was hard for him to travel. But he

needed first hand information about the country. He asked Eleanor to be his eyes and ears—and especially his legs.

Eleanor had overcome her shyness. She gladly tackled the job. No other first lady ever worked so closely with her husband.

"I've heard that there is terrible poverty in the mining towns of West Virginia," Franklin said to Eleanor. "I want you to go there and then come back and tell me the truth."

Eleanor was shocked at what she saw in West Virginia. Some of the men had been out of work for years. Even those with jobs were paid only a few dollars a week.

Eleanor visited many of the poor people. There were six children in one of the families. The father said he had only a dollar a week to feed them. Eleanor noticed that the children ate scraps out of a bowl, just like dogs.

As she left Eleanor saw a little boy holding a pet rabbit in his arms.

"What a cute rabbit!" she said. The boy seemed afraid.

His older sister said, "He thinks we are not going to eat it. But we'll have to." The boy ran out of the house, holding his rabbit tight against his chest.

When Eleanor returned to Washington she told this story at a White House dinner. The next day she received a check from one of the guests. A note said the check was to help save the rabbit.

Eleanor did everything she could to help other people. She made a lot of money by writing a newspaper column called "My Day." She gave most of the money to the poor.

She told her husband how she thought he could help. Some of his ideas for ending the depression came from her.

Not everybody liked Mrs. Roosevelt. Some people thought she should stay home in the White House and mind her own business. But she felt that helping the people was her business. She took a special interest in youth groups.

Millions of Americans loved Mrs. Roosevelt. She seemed to be everywhere all the time. Her heart was big enough for all the people in the world.

A story is told about a little girl who had heard a great deal about Mrs. Roosevelt, but had never seen her. The girl's mother took her to the Statue of Liberty one day.

"Do you know who that is?" her mother asked, pointing to the giant statue.

"Of course," the little girl replied. "That's Mrs. Roosevelt."

Chapter 8

Third Term

Mrs. Roosevelt was now a very fine politician. She was a good public speaker and she made friends easily. She helped her husband run for re-election in 1936. One important man called her "the most practical woman I've ever met in politics."

Roosevelt was re-elected by one of the greatest majorities in American history.

One Republican said, "It isn't fair for the President to cash in on his own popularity and his wife's, too."

Most Americans were proud of the Roosevelts when the King and Queen of England came to visit them. Mrs. Roosevelt planned to have a picnic for them at Hyde Park.

"What are you going to serve?" a reporter asked.

"Probably hot dogs," Eleanor said.

Many people thought hot dogs were not fancy enough for a King and Queen. But Mrs. Roosevelt went on with her plans. Someone told her that the King had never eaten a hot dog, but that he would like to try one.

At the picnic the King and Queen ate hot dogs and seemed to like them. Afterwards the President and the King went swimming while the Queen and Eleanor talked about their children.

The visit of the King and Queen helped America and England become firm friends. A few months later World War II started. England was fighting Germany.

No one was sure whether or not America could keep out of the war. Because of the war Roosevelt decided to run for a third term as President.

In all American history no President had ever served more than two terms. There was no law against it, but many people thought it would be wrong.

During the campaign Eleanor was criticized by many Republicans. Some of them wore big buttons which said "We don't want Eleanor either."

Someone asked Eleanor how she felt about the buttons. She laughed. "If I could be worried about mudslinging I would have been dead long ago."

Roosevelt was easily elected for a third term. But he made many enemies. Some people tried to strike at him through Mrs. Roosevelt.

Once, after making a speech, she said she would be glad to answer questions.

"Mrs. Roosevelt," a man said, "do you think your husband's being a cripple has affected his mind?"

The man was trying to insult Mrs. Roosevelt, but she refused to be insulted.

"Yes," she said, "my husband's illness has affected him. . . . Suffering has made him more sensitive, more responsive to his fellow men."

Mrs. Roosevelt's quiet dignity won her more friends than ever.

Chapter *9*

World War II

On December 7, 1941, Japanese planes bombed American ships in Hawaii. Japan, Italy and Germany declared war on the United States. Now America was in World War II.

All four of Mrs. Roosevelt's sons were in the armed forces. She was worried about them. But she knew the war had to be fought and won.

Queen Elizabeth asked Mrs. Roosevelt to come to England to see what English women were doing to win the war. The President thought this was a good idea.

Eleanor could visit American troops who were training in England.

Mrs. Roosevelt flew to Ireland, took a boat to England and a train to London. The King and Queen met her at the railroad station and took her to Buckingham Palace.

The dinner at the Palace that night was served on gold and silver plates. But food was scarce in England and the meal was simple.

The King and Queen took Eleanor on a trip around London. She saw many buildings that had been wrecked by German bombs.

Some people thought the Germans might try to kill Mrs. Roosevelt if they knew she was in England. So she was given a secret name. It was "Rover."

Mrs. Roosevelt's son, Elliot, was at an airfield near London. A man drove Mrs. Roosevelt to see him. On the way they got lost. Someone with them called the American Embassy in London.

He said, "Rover has lost her pup." The Embassy gave him directions and Rover had a joyful visit with her "pup."

Mrs. Roosevelt visited English factories where women were making bombs and airplanes. She went to see American soldiers who were in training camps. They cheered when they saw her.

The next year Mrs. Roosevelt went to the South Pacific. She visited homesick soldiers in hospitals.

She signed her name on many bandages and casts. She wrote down the names of mothers, sweethearts and wives, and promised to telephone them when she returned to America.

After she talked to one soldier he turned to a friend. "Jeepers! She's just like your own mother."

Mrs. Roosevelt visited a cemetery on Guadalcanal where American soldiers were buried. She made up her mind that when the war was over she would work for lasting peace. "I kept praying that I might be able to prevent . . . this stupidity called war," she said later.

When she returned to Washington she spent many hours calling friends and relatives of soldiers she had met.

One soldier had given her a message for the girl he planned to marry. Mrs. Roosevelt called and said, "This is Mrs. Roosevelt."

"Don't be funny," the girl said. "Who do you think you're fooling?" The girl would not believe it wasn't a joke. Mrs. Roosevelt finally had to write her a note.

President Roosevelt had worked long and hard for his country. He was tired. But he wanted to serve until the war was won. Then he wanted to help organize the United Nations. He hoped it would prevent future wars.

So he ran for a fourth term as President and was elected.

The next spring he went to Warm Springs, Georgia, for a rest. Mrs. Roosevelt stayed in Washington.

One day when she was away from the White House she got a message asking her to return at once. When she reached the White House she was told that her husband had died suddenly.

Mrs. Roosevelt did not think of herself. The country came first. She sent for Vice-President Harry Truman. He would now be the President.

"Harry, the President is dead," she told him.

"Is there anything I can do for you?" Truman asked.

"Is there anything we can do for you?" Mrs. Roosevelt answered. *"For you are the one in trouble now."*

Mrs. Roosevelt's job in the White House was finished. She had been first lady for more than twelve years. No other woman had ever been America's first lady for so long.

Chapter **10**

First Lady of the World

Late in 1945, President Truman asked Mrs. Roosevelt to be a United States delegate to the new United Nations. She accepted. She thought the United Nations was man's only hope for peace.

Mrs. Roosevelt was made chairman of the United Nations Commission for Human Rights. Her job was to help write a bill of rights for the people of the world.

A Russian member of the Commission liked to make long speeches and slow the work down. Once he accused the United States of doing bad things.

Mrs. Roosevelt banged on the table for order. *"We are here,"* she said sternly, *"to devise ways of safeguarding human rights. We are not here to attack each others' governments. . . ."*

Finally the bill was finished. It was called the Declaration of Human Rights. When it was passed by the United Nations, all the delegates stood up and cheered Mrs. Roosevelt. People began to call her the First Lady of the World.

Mrs. Roosevelt also worked for the American Association for the United Nations. It tried to make Americans support the United Nations.

"It is not perfect," she said, "but it is all we have." As long as men argued with words, she thought, they would not fight with bullets.

Once she went to Russia and talked with Nikita Khrushchev, the head of the Russian government. They argued about many things.

As she left he asked, "Can I tell our papers that we had a friendly conversation?"

"You can say that we had a friendly conversation, but that we differ," she told him.

"At least we didn't shoot each other," the Russian said with a grin.

Mrs. Roosevelt traveled all over the world in the cause of peace. People everywhere loved her.

Strangers would come up and shake her hand. "Hi, Eleanor," they would say. They were proud to meet her.

Mrs. Roosevelt was busy each day from breakfast to bedtime. She answered every letter she received—and there were thousands. She made speeches and wrote books. She helped the needy. And she helped the Democratic party.

Her friends tried to make her stop working so hard. But she wouldn't stop. "There's so much to do," she said.

In the fall of 1962 Mrs. Roosevelt became sick and went to a hospital. Everybody was worried about her.

People felt better when she was able to leave the hospital and go home. But suddenly she became ill again. She died on November 7.

The whole world mourned. Many people who had never met her felt that they had lost a good friend.

The United Nations stopped its work in her honor. One of her great admirers made a speech. *"Her glow has warmed the world,"* he said.